COLORADO

AVALANCHE

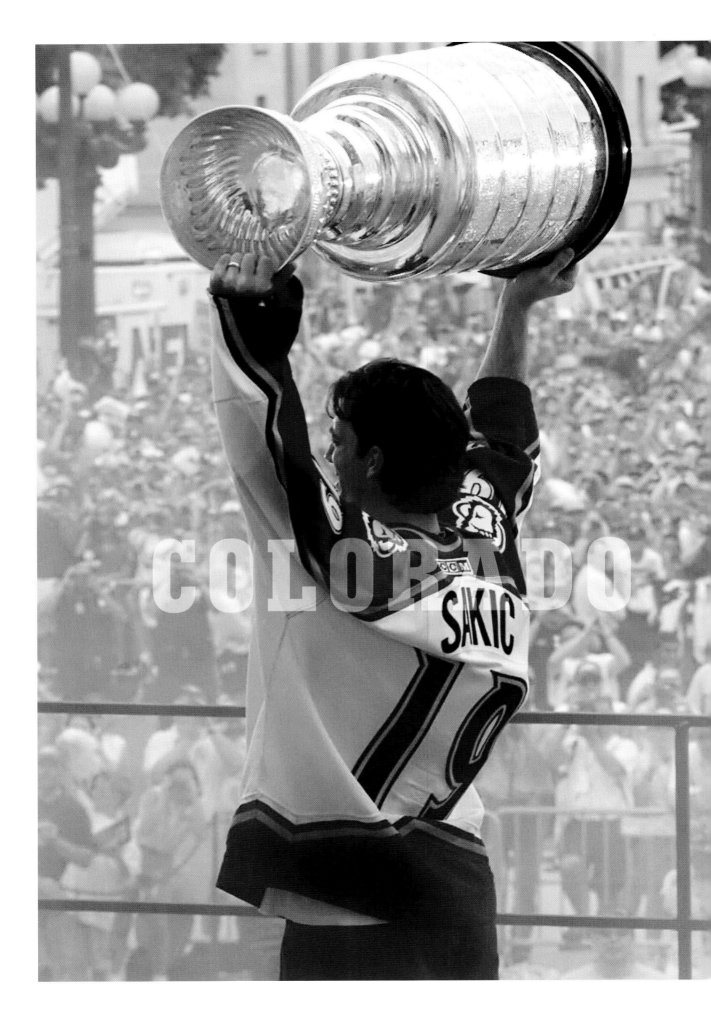

THE COLORADO AVALANCHE HAD JUST BEATEN THE
NEW JERSEY DEVILS TO WIN THE 2001 STANLEY
CUP, AND THE CELEBRATION WAS ON. AT MID-ICE IN
DENVER'S PEPSI CENTER, CENTER JOE SAKIC RAISED
THE BIG SILVER CHALICE FIRST. SAKIC, THE TEAM'S
CAPTAIN, HAD STARRED WITH THE CLUB SINCE 1988,
WHEN IT PLAYED IN QUEBEC CITY, QUEBEC, AS THE
NORDIQUES. SAKIC THEN HANDED THE THREE-FOOT (91
CM) TROPHY TO A PLAYER WHO HAD BEEN WITH THE
TEAM FOR ONLY A YEAR: 40-YEAR-OLD DEFENSEMAN
RAY BOURQUE. IN HIS LONG CAREER, BOURQUE HAD

NEVER HOISTED THE STANLEY CUP, AND THE DENVER
CROWD RESPONDED WITH AN EMOTIONAL ROAR FOR
THE OLD NEWCOMER. "JUST SEEING RAY CARRY THAT
CUP AROUND THE ICE MAKES YOU WANT TO CRY," SAID
AVALANCHE WING DAN HINOTE. "IT MAKES EVERY-
THING IN THE WORLD SEEM RIGHT AGAIN." FOR THE
SECOND TIME IN THEIR FIRST SIX SEASONS IN DENVER,
THE AVALANCHE WERE KINGS OF THE HOCKEY WORLD.

THREE CITIES, TWO LEAGUES

DENVER, COLORADO, SITS IN AN UNLIKELY place. The city is walled off by 14,000-foot (4,270 m) mountains to the west and faces vast, dry prairies to the east. Denver was built by gold prospectors who put down roots there in 1858. By the late 1800s, the city had become a railroad, banking, and commercial center, and was the second-largest city in the West, behind only San Francisco. Since 1863, it's been home to a branch of the United States mint, which produces U.S. coins. Today, this city of half a million people boasts a thriving tourism industry, attracting skiers and hikers to those once-forbidding mountains, and is home to professional teams in the four major sports of baseball, football, basketball, and hockey.

Denver has a rich hockey history that includes an NHL team called the Rockies, which played in the "Mile-High City" from 1976 to 1982.

The hockey franchise that would eventually become the Colorado Avalanche began as San Francisco's entry in the World Hockey Association (WHA), a new rival to the long-established National Hockey League (NHL), in 1972. But before the team played a single game on the California coast, it was purchased for $215,000 by a group of businessmen from Quebec City that included Paul Racine and Jean Lesage. They named the team the Nordiques, a French word meaning "Northerners," because French-speaking Quebec City was one of the league's northernmost cities. The team's uniforms sported the fleur-de-lis, the centuries-old symbol of French influence.

Maurice "Rocket" Richard, a former Montreal Canadiens wing who had been the first player ever to score 50 goals in an NHL season, was named the team's first coach in 1972, but he would coach only one game before deciding that the job wasn't for him. The Nordiques would endure eight coaching changes in their first nine seasons but become a consistent force on the ice.

AVALANCHE ALL-TIME TEAM

Joe Sakic CENTER

Known for his wicked wrist shot, Joe Sakic was as much of a symbol of the Colorado Avalanche as the A on the team's sweaters. Going into the 2007–08 season, he had played 18 seasons with the franchise, assisting on a goal in his first game with the Quebec Nordiques in 1988 and topping the franchise career scoring list with 610 goals through 2006–07. Sakic grew up speaking Croatian in Vancouver, British Columbia, picked up English in school, and then had to learn French in Quebec. He scored an NHL-record six game-winning goals in the 1996 playoffs. Sakic wore number 19 his entire hockey life, from pee-wee league to the NHL.

NORDIQUES/AVALANCHE SEASONS: 1988–present
HEIGHT: 5-11 (180 cm)
WEIGHT: 195 (88 kg)

- NHL-record 7 overtime playoff goals
- 1996 Conn Smythe Trophy winner (as playoffs MVP)
- 14-time All-Star
- 2001 Hart Trophy winner (as league MVP)

French-Canadian wing Marc Tardif spent four seasons with the Montreal Canadiens before becoming a high-scoring star for the Quebec Nordiques.

In the Nordiques' first season, they signed star Montreal defenseman J. C. Tremblay, and he promptly led the new WHA in assists with 75. In 1975, the Nordiques reached the AVCO World Trophy Finals—the league's championship series—but were swept by the Houston Aeros. In 1975–76, Quebec wing Marc Tardif scored 71 goals, and the next season, forward Real Cloutier poured in 66 goals as the Nordiques won the AVCO Cup, defeating the Winnipeg Jets in seven games. More success followed in 1977–78, as Tardif was named league Most Valuable Player (MVP).

"My dad played with the best and he was one of the best. Every day, I learned something new. Every game he watched me, he gave me a tip to be better."

COLORADO CENTER PAUL STASTNY,
ON HIS FATHER PETER

By 1979, many of the WHA's teams were struggling financially, and the two major leagues, tired of competing against one another, merged. Four WHA teams, including the Nordiques, joined the older NHL, instantly expanding the league and deepening its pool of talent.

The Nordiques struggled in their first year in the NHL, finishing last in the Wales Conference's five-team Adams Division. But through a risky piece of international intrigue, the club was about to make headlines.

The Czech Brothers

Peter (left), Marian (middle), and Anton Stastny

PETER, ANTON, AND MARIAN STASTNY, three brothers from Czechoslovakia, made the Quebec Nordiques a family force in the NHL in the 1980s. On February 20, 1981, Peter and Anton both scored hat tricks (three goals) in a game against the Vancouver Canucks, and two days later, the brothers repeated the feat against the Washington Capitals. That season, Peter set an NHL rookie record with 70 assists. The next year, after older brother Marian joined the team, Peter posted 139 points (46 goals plus 93 assists)—still a franchise record. The three brothers combined for 233 points during the 1983–84 season, in which the Nordiques set a franchise record with 977 points. Peter and Anton Stastny today rank third and fourth respectively in the Quebec-Colorado record book for career goals. The family's impact on the franchise continues today. Peter Stastny's son, Paul, a center, took the ice for the Avalanche in the 2006–07 season. He wore number 62 on his sweater that season but later changed it to 26, his father's number. His teammate, center Joe Sakic, had played with his father and uncle Anton in Quebec. "It's a pretty cool feeling," Paul Stastny said. Paul's brother, Yan, broke into the NHL with the Boston Bruins in 2006.

12

CZECH MATES

IN 1979, THE NORDIQUES DRAFTED CZECH wing Anton Stastny. But because his country, Czechoslovakia, was ruled by communism, a political system that prevented its citizens from moving freely, Stastny was stuck. In the summer of 1980, Nordiques team officials went to Innsbruck, Austria, to watch the European Cup tournament. But their true intent was to help Anton Stastny and his brother Peter, a center, make their escape. Secretly staying at the same hotel as the Stastnys, Nordiques president Marcel Aubut and director of player development Gilles Leger sneaked the brothers and Peter's wife Darina to Vienna, Austria, where they signed papers making their escape official.

Peter Stastny emerged as the greatest of the three Stastny brothers, becoming the second-best scorer in the NHL in the 1980s (after Wayne Gretzky).

The next season, center Jacques Richard scored 52 goals for the Nordiques, the Stastnys each scored 39, and Peter won the Calder Trophy as the NHL's Rookie of the Year. Older brother Marian, a wing, joined them for the 1981–82 season. Although Marian would play only four years, the three brothers would score a combined 730 goals in their Nordiques careers. Along with wing Michel Goulet, they made the Nordiques a fearsome scoring machine. "They are all so quick and good with the puck," said Boston Bruins defenseman Brad Park. "Throw in Goulet and there may as well be four brothers."

In 1982–83, under the leadership of coach Michel Bergeron, Goulet netted a career-high 57, Peter Stastny 47, Marian Stastny 36, and Anton Stastny 32. The next season, the Nordiques would score 360 goals, setting a franchise record that still stands. While the scoring frenzy delighted fans at the Colisée de Quebec, the Nordiques' home arena, it wasn't enough to compensate for a weak defense. The Nordiques finished fourth in the Adams Division in 1982–83 and were knocked out of the playoffs by Boston in the first round.

"I try to hit them before they hit me. It's easier."

QUEBEC/COLORADO CENTER PETER FORSBERG, ON THE NHL'S PHYSICAL PLAY

Despite their high-scoring nucleus, the Nordiques would win their division only once during the 1980s—in 1985–86, when they lost in the first round of the playoffs to the Hartford Whalers. They fought their way to the Wales Conference Finals twice: in 1982, when they were swept by the New York Islanders, and in 1985, when they fell to the Philadelphia Flyers.

Classy, tough, and respected by teammates and foes alike, Michel Goulet scored at least 20 goals in each of the first 14 seasons of his NHL career.

One of the reasons for the team's struggles is that it often played short-handed; many Nordiques players showed a lack of self-discipline and ended up in the penalty box for fighting or other infractions. In the early 1980s, rough-and-tumble center Dale Hunter spent a franchise-playoff-record 357 minutes in the "sin bin," and in 1987–88, defenseman Gord Donnelly set a team single-season record with 301 penalty minutes. Nordiques players would watch the playoffs from home every spring from 1988 to 1992 as their high-scoring flashes of success in the 1970s and early '80s faded into memory.

If there was a silver lining to the dark clouds that settled over the Nordiques, it was that the team's poor records consistently gave it early selections in the annual NHL Draft. In 1987, Quebec selected center Joe Sakic, a Vancouver native who would soon prove himself one of the game's elite players. In the 1989–90 season, Sakic would become the first player in NHL history to score 100 points

Peter Forsberg WING

Peter Forsberg joined Quebec in a stunning 1992 trade that sent unsigned number-one draft pick Eric Lindros to the Philadelphia Flyers for Forsberg, five other players, two draft picks, and $15 million. After the Quebec Nordiques became the Colorado Avalanche, Forsberg helped Colorado capture two Stanley Cups. Forsberg combined European-style speed and stick-handling ability with a North American-style combativeness. He quickly became one of the most prolific scorers in team history, despite suffering numerous injuries. He appeared on a postage stamp in Sweden after scoring a gold-medal-winning shootout goal for his homeland in the 1994 Winter Olympics.

NORDIQUES/AVALANCHE SEASONS: 1994–2004
HEIGHT: 6-0 (183 cm)
WEIGHT: 205 (93 kg)

- 1995 Calder Trophy winner (as Rookie of the Year)
- 5-time All-Star
- 2003 Art Ross Trophy winner (as NHL points leader)
- 2003 Hart Trophy winner

The Nordiques were a formidable team in the early '80s, reaching the conference finals in 1982 and 1985, but were frequently penalized for fighting.

(goals plus assists) for a team with the worst record in the league.

In the 1989 Draft, the Nordiques made two more shrewd additions, selecting center Mats Sundin with the first overall pick and shoring up their defense by taking defenseman Adam Foote. Then, in 1991, again picking first, Quebec drafted towering center Eric Lindros. Nordiques fans were thrilled; Lindros had been dubbed "The Next One" and was widely hailed as the greatest pro hockey prospect to come along in years. Lindros would indeed have an enormous impact on the Nordiques, but not in the way expected.

"I remember when I was in grade nine, my dad told me that I should take French, and I told him that I would never need it. As soon as I got drafted by the Quebec Nordiques, he said, 'See, I told you.'"

QUEBEC/COLORADO DEFENSEMAN ADAM FOOTE

Breaking 50

Jacques Richard

FIFTY GOALS IN A SEASON HAS LONG been a celebrated achievement for an NHL player, and it's a feat that helps to put fans in the seats. But breaking 50 doesn't guarantee championships. Jacques Richard netted 52 goals in 1980–81 in Quebec, becoming the first player in franchise history to do so. The feat was a shocking one; Richard had been a prolific scorer in junior hockey, but, aside from that 52-goal season for the Nordiques, he never scored more than 27 in 10 other NHL seasons. In Richard's big season, the Nordiques lost more games than they won and finished in fourth place in the Adams Division. Hall of Fame winger Michel Goulet scored more than 50 goals in four straight seasons (1982–83 to 1985–86) for the Quebec Nordiques, including the franchise record of 57 in 1982–83. But the team captured only one Adams Division championship during that stretch. On the other hand, center Joe Sakic broke the prestigious mark with 51 goals in 1995–96 and a career-high 54 in 2000–01, and the Avalanche won the Stanley Cup both years. The last Avs player to "light the lamp" 50 times in a season was wing Milan Hejduk, who did so in 2002–03, helping make the Avalanche division champs again.

THE LINDROS EFFECT

LINDROS MADE HEADLINES ACROSS THE SPORTS world—and caused outrage among Quebec fans—by refusing to sign with the struggling Nordiques. When Lindros still refused after being offered a 10-year, $50-million contract, even Canadian prime minister Brian Mulroney publicly scolded the 18-year-old. Lindros wouldn't budge, however, sitting out a full NHL season and giving the Nordiques little choice but to trade him. In 1992, the Philadelphia Flyers took Lindros off the Nordiques' hands in a blockbuster trade that sent All-Star goalie Ron Hextall, a young Swedish center named Peter Forsberg, four other players, two first-round draft picks, and $15 million to Quebec. The Nordiques were pleased with the swap. "Eric is a great player," said Nordiques coach and general manager Pierre Page, "but we needed more than one great player to turn our team around."

Although drafted six spots behind Eric Lindros in 1991, seven-time All-Star Peter Forsberg would go on to have the more successful career.

Forsberg would play two years in his native Sweden before suiting up for Quebec. The Nordiques had a flicker of success without him in 1992–93, assembling a 47-27-10 record and making the playoffs. But in 1993–94, they slumped back to fifth in their division.

Pierre Page was fired in 1994, and Pierre Lacroix, a player agent who had once played for the Nordiques, replaced him as general manager. Lacroix quickly filled the team's coaching vacancy with Marc Crawford, a former Vancouver Canucks player and minor-league coach with a reputation as a fiery disciplinarian. More significantly, Lacroix managed to get Forsberg onto the ice in Colisée de Quebec, signing him to a contract before the 1994–95 season.

That season was delayed by a labor dispute between players and owners, but the new-look Nordiques then dashed to a division title with a 30-13-5 record. Unfortunately, the Nordiques fizzled in the playoffs, losing in the

Michel Goulet WING

Born in Peribonca, Quebec, Michel Goulet was the first player to sign an NHL contract written entirely in French. An offensive star who developed stout defensive skills as a pro, Goulet played with the Birmingham Bulls of the World Hockey Association before joining the Quebec Nordiques in the NHL. In 11 seasons, he scored 456 goals for the Nordiques. Despite earning many individual accolades, Goulet never played on a Stanley Cup winner. He was inducted into the Hockey Hall of Fame along with former Nordiques teammate Peter Stastny in 1998, and he remains with the Avalanche today as a team executive.

NORDIQUES SEASONS: 1979–90
HEIGHT: 6-0 (183 cm)
WEIGHT: 185 (84 kg)

- Scored 50 or more goals in 4 seasons
- Team-record 57 goals in 1982–83
- 5-time All-Star
- Hockey Hall of Fame inductee (1998)

During his four seasons as coach of the Nordiques/Avalanche, Marc Crawford led the franchise to four division titles and one Stanley Cup.

first round to the New York Rangers. Worse yet, Nordiques fans were about to lose their franchise.

The first years of the 1990s had been difficult ones for the Nordiques. Quebec was by far the smallest of all NHL cities, and the team played in a stadium that did not feature the expensive "luxury box" seats found in many other arenas. As a result, the club's owners struggled to afford the high salaries it took to obtain the best players. Team president Marcel Aubut asked the Quebec provincial government in 1994 to help the team pay for a new stadium, but his pleas fell on unsympathetic ears. "I have more important things to deal with than Mr. Aubut's every little twitch," Quebec premier Jacques Parizeau replied.

"For a little boy from Quebec, I never thought this all would happen. Not even when I was playing ball hockey. I never thought it could happen."

COLORADO GOALTENDER PATRICK ROY, AFTER WINNING HIS FOURTH STANLEY CUP

So it was not much of a surprise in Quebec in the spring of 1995 when COMSAT Entertainment Group, a hotel video company that also owned pro basketball's Denver Nuggets, bought the hockey franchise for $75 million and announced it would move the team to Denver. After 23 years, NHL hockey in Quebec had come to an end.

Architect of the Avalanche

Patrick Roy   Pierre Lacroix

PIERRE LACROIX WAS NAMED GENERAL manager of the Nordiques in 1994. He took over a team that had missed the NHL playoffs in six of the previous seven seasons and was in serious financial trouble. He quickly hired Marc Crawford as coach, and the Nordiques won their division in 1994–95. A year later, when the franchise was sold, moved to Colorado, and renamed, Lacroix began building around young players such as centers Peter Forsberg and Joe Sakic. He traded for tough wing Claude Lemieux and Montreal Canadiens goalie Patrick Roy (pronounced *ruh-WAH*), who many thought was past his prime. That loaded Avalanche roster captured the Stanley Cup in its first season in Denver. After several more seasons that produced division championships but no Stanley Cups, Lacroix bolstered the defense with Ray Bourque and Rob Blake. In 2000–01, the Avalanche enjoyed their best regular-season ever and won their second Stanley Cup. Under Lacroix's direction, the Nordiques–Avalanche won nine straight division championships, went to the Western Conference Finals six times, and raised the Cup twice. Lacroix was replaced as general manager in May 2006 but remained president of the Avalanche. "I'm going to do everything I can to make sure this team wins for another decade," Lacroix said.

AU REVOIR, QUEBEC; HELLO, STANLEY CUP

DENVER SPORTS FANS RESPONDED TO the relocation enthusiastically. Even though Colorado governor Roy Romer struggled to pronounce "Sakic" when greeting the team in May 1995 (saying "Kasic" instead), fans bought 12,000 season tickets in a little more than a month after the sale and move was announced. "We're bringing winners into Denver," COMSAT president Charlie Lyons promised.

Renamed the Colorado Avalanche, the club beat the defending Western Conference champion Detroit Red Wings, 3–2, in its first game on October 6, 1995. (The NHL had been split into Eastern and Western Conferences in 1993.) Two months later, Pierre Lacroix

Joe Sakic was outstanding during the team's first season in Colorado, scoring 51 goals during the regular season, then another 18 in the playoffs.

announced one of the most stunning NHL trades in years, sending goalten-der Jocelyn Thibault and two other players to Montreal for All-Star goalie Patrick Roy. Suddenly, the team appeared stacked with talent: it had electri-fying scoring threats in Sakic, Forsberg, and wings Claude Lemieux and Valeri Kamensky; a disruptive defense led by Foote, Uwe Krupp, Chris Simon, and Sandis Ozolinsh; and arguably the game's best puck-stopper in the nets.

Forsberg exploded for a career-high 116 points in 1995–96, and the Avalanche won the Pacific Division championship. The "Avs" then threw Colorado sports fans into a state of euphoria as they streaked all the way to the 1996 Stanley Cup Finals, turning back the Vancouver Canucks and the Chicago Blackhawks in the first two rounds of the playoffs and upsetting Detroit in the Western Conference Finals. Facing the three-year-old Florida Panthers in the Cup Finals, the Avalanche won the first three games, but in Game 4,

Rob Blake DEFENSEMAN

The soft-spoken but hard-hitting Blake was born in Simcoe, Ontario, where his parents were tobacco and strawberry farmers. He played 12 seasons with the Los Angeles Kings before being traded to the Colorado Avalanche in March 2001. After the Avalanche won the Stanley Cup that May, Blake brought the trophy back to Simcoe and showed it off to neighbors from atop the family combine. "I grew up skating on a pond next to the farm, so to be able to bring it home is special," he said. "The look on my dad's face when they lifted it out of the box was priceless."

AVALANCHE SEASONS: 2001–06
HEIGHT: 6-4 (193 cm)
WEIGHT: 225 (102 kg)

- 1998 Norris Trophy winner (as best defenseman)
- Career-high 23 goals in 1997–98
- 6-time All-Star
- Scored 19 points in the 2001 playoffs

Considered by some the greatest goalie in NHL history, Patrick Roy was famous for his confident attitude and unshakeable concentration in the nets.

the Panthers fought Colorado to a scoreless tie through three periods, one overtime, and then through another overtime. Finally, in the third overtime and just after 1:00 A.M., Uwe Krupp fired the puck past Florida goalie John Vanbiesbrouck to clinch the Stanley Cup for Colorado.

Almost 500,000 people turned out near Colorado's state capitol for a victory parade and ceremony. While celebrating with the team's new crowd, coach Marc Crawford also gratefully acknowledged the club's roots and fans in Quebec City. "I would like them to feel included in our victory," he said. "We lived in a marvelous hockey town, and we've been lucky to be welcomed in another."

"It's a little like the guy who sees the love of his life marry someone else."

FORMER QUEBEC TEAM TRAINER JACQUES LAVERGNE, AFTER THE AVALANCHE WON THE STANLEY CUP IN THEIR FIRST YEAR IN COLORADO

The 1996–97 Avalanche repeated as Pacific Division champs and advanced past Chicago and the Edmonton Oilers to again meet the Detroit Red Wings in the Western Conference Finals. But the Red Wings gained some retribution, stopping the Avalanche in six games and then winning the Stanley Cup for themselves.

In 1997–98, Colorado again won its division, but this time it exited the postseason even sooner, losing to Edmonton in the first round. As the club's 1996 title began to seem distant, Lacroix began making moves he hoped would put the Avalanche back on top.

Finding a Name

WHEN THE QUEBEC NORDIQUES WERE purchased by COMSAT Entertainment Group in 1995, it was clear that the team would need a new name. Nordiques means "Northerners," and that certainly didn't describe Denver. At first, the new owners wanted to call the team the Rocky Mountain Extreme, but the Colorado public didn't like that. So when players such as Joe Sakic, Peter Forsberg, and Adam Deadmarsh arrived at a ceremony to meet their new fans in the spring of 1995, they wore plain white T-shirts with "Colorado NHL" printed on the front. The owners set up a "feedback forum" in which fans could identify their preference for a new name: Black Bears, Outlaws, Wranglers, Rapids, Renegades, Storm, Cougars, or Avalanche. "Cougars" won out in the fan voting, but the owners had the final say and decided on "Avalanche." The name was unique in all of professional sports, describing the dangerous snow slides that can occur in mountainous areas such as Colorado. The team lived up to its new name, rolling over all challengers in its first season in Denver to win the Pacific Division championship, the Western Conference championship, and the Stanley Cup.

REBUILDING
IN THE ROCKIES

LACROIX FIRED CRAWFORD IN 1998 AND replaced him with Bob Hartley, a successful coach from the minor leagues. Lacroix also added wing Milan Hejduk—who had just helped the Czech Republic team win gold in the Winter Olympics—and found a roster spot for wing Chris Drury, a star on Boston University's national championship team in 1995. Drury earned Rookie of the Year honors in 1998–99 as the Avalanche won their division again.

Colorado knocked off the San Jose Sharks in the first round of the playoffs, with Hejduk scoring two overtime goals (including the series-winner), becoming the first NHL rookie to do so since 1939. The Avs advanced to face the Red Wings again, this time in the Western Conference semifinals. The Avalanche dethroned the defending Stanley Cup champions in six games, only to fall to the

Durable wing Milan Hejduk came to Colorado with Olympic experience and soon developed into one of the game's highest-scoring players.

Dallas Stars in seven hard-fought games in the Western Conference Finals. Despite the addition of wing Alex Tanguay, the Avs' following season ended in identical fashion, with a Game 7 loss to the Stars in the conference finals.

Toward the end of that 1999–2000 season, Lacroix traded for Boston Bruins defenseman Ray Bourque. In 21 seasons in the NHL, Bourque had won the Norris Trophy as the league's best defenseman five times, but he had never played for a Stanley Cup winner. At the start of the 2000–01 season, his 22nd, he asked his new teammates to commit themselves to winning a championship. They responded with the best season in franchise history, winning 52 regular-season games. Late in the season, Lacroix traded wing Adam Deadmarsh to the Los Angeles Kings for veteran defenseman Rob Blake, and Colorado was loaded for another run at the Stanley Cup. Bourque called it "Mission 16W"—16 playoff wins, and the Stanley Cup would belong to Colorado.

Adam Foote DEFENSEMAN

Adam Foote was a Toronto Maple Leafs fan as a boy, but when he finally donned a blue sweater in the NHL, it was that of the Quebec Nordiques. The defenseman moved to Colorado with the franchise in 1995 and was one of only six players to skate for both of Colorado's Stanley Cup-winning teams. For eight years, he not only protected Patrick Roy around the goal but was also Roy's roommate. Tough and durable, Foote played one 2003 play-off game with a foot fracture. In 2002, he helped Team Canada win its first Olympic gold medal since 1952.

NORDIQUES/AVALANCHE SEASONS: 1991–2004
HEIGHT: 6-1 (185 cm)
WEIGHT: 202 (92 kg)

- Played in 154 playoff games for the Nordiques/ Avalanche
- Career-high 11 goals in 2002–03
- 3-time member of Canadian Olympic team
- Career-high 168 penalty minutes in 1992–93

Although Ray Bourque had lost some speed by the time he joined the Avalanche, his inspirational leadership helped Colorado capture the 2001 Cup.

The Avalanche swept Vancouver in the opening round, held off Los Angeles in seven games in the conference semifinals, and rolled over the St. Louis Blues in five games to reach the Stanley Cup Finals against the New Jersey Devils. But Colorado would have to take the ice without Forsberg, who had suffered a mysterious and potentially life-threatening spleen rupture after the Los Angeles series.

After six tense games, the series was tied as it moved to Denver for the deciding Game 7. Bourque gave his teammates a pep talk, reminding them that championship opportunities are rare—he'd played 1,825 NHL games without having won a title. With the capacity Pepsi Center crowd roaring for the Stanley Cup's return, Tanguay scored goals in both the first and second periods. Sakic added an insurance goal, and the Avalanche won 3–1 to capture their second Stanley Cup in six seasons. "There is no way to compare this with the last Cup," Lacroix said. "Everyone who has ever won multiple championships has told me that a repeat is so difficult, and I believe them. I now know how hard it is."

"It was more or less relief rather than exhilaration or excitement. You're so tired and so happy at the same time."

COLORADO DEFENSEMAN UWE KRUPP,
ON WINNING THE 1996 STANLEY CUP

A High-Stakes Rivalry

Claude Lemieux

FEW RIVALRIES IN SPORTS HAVE EVER matched the intensity of the seven-year feud that raged between the Colorado Avalanche and the Detroit Red Wings from 1996 to 2002. The bad blood began in the 1996 Western Conference Finals, when the Avalanche upset the Red Wings in six games en route to their first Stanley Cup. In the final game of that series, Avalanche wing Claude Lemieux checked Red Wings center Kris Draper from behind, breaking Draper's nose, jaw, and cheekbone, and leaving him with cuts that needed 40 stitches to close. Toward the end of the next season, Detroit wing Darren McCarty decked Lemieux as part of a brawl in which even the teams' goalies went at each other. The Red Wings got further revenge when they beat the Avalanche in a six-game rematch in the conference finals that year and went on to win the Cup themselves. Colorado bumped Detroit from the conference semifinals in both 1999 and 2000, but in 2002, the Red Wings beat the Avalanche in the conference finals and went on to win the Stanley Cup. "We all took some bumps and bruises in the rivalry," said Claude Lemieux. "That's what made it what it was."

DEFENDING THE CUP

BOURQUE RETIRED JUST TWO WEEKS AFTER THE championship, but the rest of the Avalanche set out to defend their title. Roy posted a career-best 1.94 goals-against average (GAA) in 2001–02, and center Steven Reinprecht, picked up from the Los Angeles Kings, scored a career-high 19 goals. Forsberg sat out the regular season with injuries but returned for the 2002 playoffs and led the Avalanche back to the Western Conference Finals. In yet another show-down with the rival Red Wings, Forsberg scored an overtime goal in Game 5 in Detroit, silencing the Red Wings fans and giving the Avalanche a three-games-to-two lead. But the Avalanche lost the final two games, ending their season on a bitter note.

Steven Reinprecht skated for the Avalanche for three seasons, earning a reputation as a standout power-play performer and a valuable playoff scorer.

Early in the 2002–03 season, Coach Hartley was fired and replaced by Tony Granato. Despite the change in leadership, the Avs won an NHL-record ninth straight division title. Hejduk led the NHL with 50 goals, and Forsberg won the Hart Trophy as league MVP. But the team was upset in the first round of the playoffs by the Minnesota Wild. Colorado then suffered another blow as Roy announced his retirement.

The next season, Colorado's streak of division titles ended with a second-place finish, and the team was eliminated in the second round of the play-offs. More bad news followed: Forsberg left town to join Philadelphia as a free agent, and the 2004–05 season was cancelled due to a salary dispute between players and owners. The Avs bounced back in 2005–06, as rookie wing Marek Svatos tied for the team lead with 32 goals and the team upset the Dallas Stars in the first round of the playoffs. But the Avalanche were then swept by the Mighty Ducks of Anaheim.

AVALANCHE ALL-TIME TEAM

Patrick Roy GOALIE

Patrick Roy was generally regarded as the less talented of two hockey-playing brothers who grew up in Quebec City. But when agent Pierre Lacroix came to sign forward Stephane Roy in 1984, the boys' father, Michel, insisted that Lacroix sign Patrick as well. Stephane would score one goal in a 12-game NHL career, while Patrick would become a legend. At age 20, he led the Montreal Canadiens to the 1986 Stanley Cup. Called "St. Patrick" in Montreal, Roy was traded in December 1995 to Colorado. The following spring, he led the Avalanche to the Stanley Cup and was in goal again for the team's 2001 championship five years later.

AVALANCHE SEASONS: 1995–2003
HEIGHT: 6-0 (183 cm)
WEIGHT: 165 (75 kg)

- 3-time Conn Smythe Trophy winner
- 551 career wins (most all-time)
- Stopped all 63 shots by the Florida Panthers in Game 4 of the 1996 Stanley Cup Finals
- 3-time Vezina Trophy winner (as best goaltender)

Slovakian wing Marek Svatos emerged as a rising star in 2005–06, netting 32 goals despite missing part of the season with a shoulder injury.

The 2006–07 Avalanche were a team in transition. Team president Pierre Lacroix, who had spent 12 years as general manager, was replaced by Francois Giguere. On October 16, 2006, the team's NHL-record string of 487 home sell-outs finally ended. The team finished the season in ninth place in the Western Conference and missed the playoffs for the first time since 1994, when it still played in Quebec. Still, there were reasons to believe the Avs would soon be back in contention. Center Paul Stastny scored 28 goals to emerge as one of the NHL's top rookies, and Sakic, Hejduk, and wing Wojtek Wolski contributed to a formidable offense. Defensively, goalie Peter Budaj, in his first season as the Avs' full-time netminder, built an impressive 31–16–6 record. "I think we're going to come back and pick up where we left off," said Sakic.

The story of the Colorado Avalanche is a winding one, encompassing four decades, three cities, two countries, and two leagues. And since the franchise put down roots in the Rocky Mountains, that story has come to include two Stanley Cup championships as well. For Denver fans, the "Mile-High City" skaters with the big A on their sweaters can't bring that big silver chalice back to town soon enough.

A Big Mac and Pepsi

Pepsi Center

THE QUEBEC NORDIQUES PLAYED FROM 1972 through 1995 in Colisée de Quebec, an arena built in 1949 after Quebec City's original Colisée burned down. Reconstituted in Denver in 1995 as the Colorado Avalanche, the team played four seasons in McNichols Arena, nicknamed "Big Mac." Built for $16 million, McNichols had opened in August 1975. It was then home to the NBA's Denver Nuggets, and it had hosted the 1984 NBA All-Star Game and the 1990 Final Four of men's college basketball. The Avalanche played and won the first two games of the Stanley Cup Finals there in 1996. McNichols was razed in 1999, when the Avalanche and Nuggets moved to the $160-million Pepsi Center in downtown Denver. Pepsi Center had room for 2,000 more hockey fans than McNichols did, and it featured an extra basketball floor so the Avalanche and Nuggets could practice at the same time. The arena stands in the heart of Denver. Nearby are Invesco Field at Mile High, where the Denver Broncos of the National Football League play, and Coors Field, where Major League Baseball's Colorado Rockies play. Colisée de Quebec is still used for sports and other events in Quebec City, and is known today as Colisée Pepsi.

Holding 18,000 fans for hockey games, Pepsi Center hosted Avalanche playoff games in each of the first six seasons after it opened in 1999.

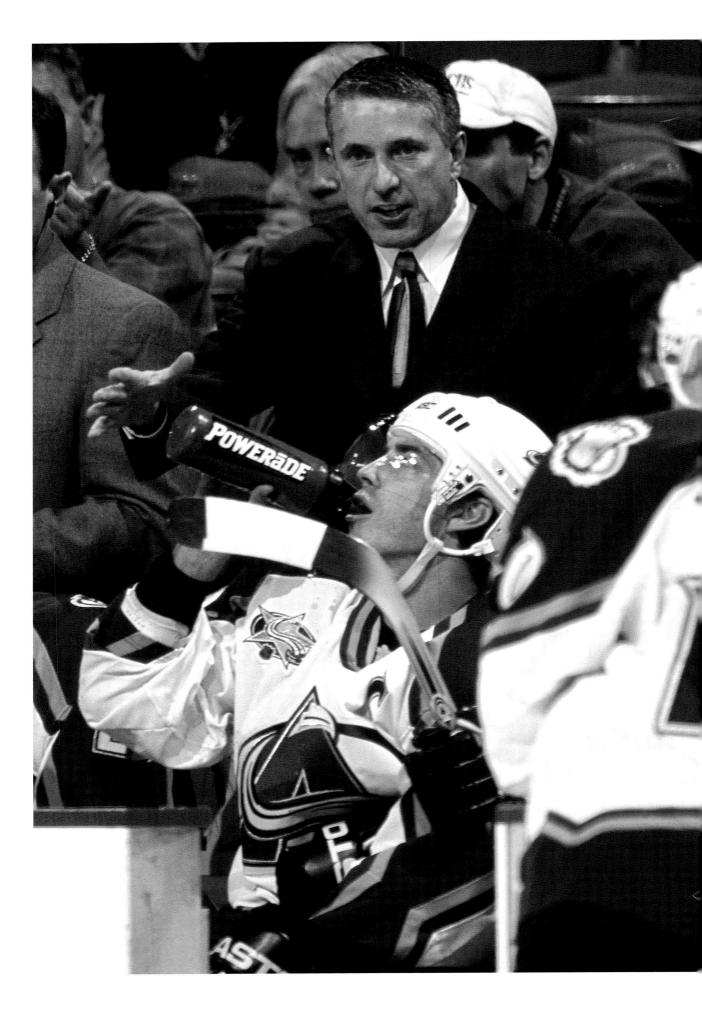

Bob Hartley COACH

After starting out as a junior hockey coach in 1987, Bob Hartley advanced through the minor-league ranks, coaching his clubs to championships at every level. Finally, in 1998, he got his big opportunity as coach of the Avalanche. His team started just 2–6–1 that season, but two seasons later, Colorado hoisted the Stanley Cup as world champion. As he won a franchise-record 193 career games with the Avs, Hartley earned an unusual reputation—that of a loud and demanding taskmaster who loved practical jokes. "He's an interesting character," said Avs wing Ville Nieminen. "He calls himself Uncle Bob. Uncle Bob knows everything. That's his line."

AVALANCHE SEASONS AS COACH: 1998–2002
NHL COACHING RECORD: 330–226–61
STANLEY CUP CHAMPIONSHIP WITH COLORADO: 2001

INDEX